To: Joe

ALONGSIDE THE [illegible]
MISSIONARIES

THERE WAS AN INDIAN

WORKING TOO

THE STORY OF RAMIRO MORRIS
Pioneer missionary from Rio Tigre, San Blas Islands, Panama

AS DICTATED IN SPANISH TO JANICE (Juanita) AND RICHARD (Ricardo) LARSON

A big thank you for helping Ramiro Morris rebuild the Church building - for his people on the San Blas Islands! This is his story!

Blessings!

Janice Larson

Author: Janice S. Larson (Juanita)

ISBN: 978-0-9974878-5-5

Other books by this author:

- Había un Indio - 2013
- He made Something Beautiful - 2016
- El Hizo Algo Bello. – 2016 (Spanish translation of He Made Something Beautiful)
- Miracles in Madrid - 2018
- Milagros en Madrid – 2018 (Spanish translation of Miracles in Madrid

Table of Contents

ALONGSIDE THE AMERICAN MISSIONARIES

THERE WAS AN INDIAN WORKING TOO

INTRODUCTION

It is with great enthusiasm and honor that we present the story of Ramiro Morris in English. It was first published in Spanish in 2013. We have known Ramiro for more then 50 years and deeply love and respect him. We lived much of this story with him.

He is a true man of God who has suffered much, but like Job, he is able to say, **"It was all in the plan of God!"**

Ramiro is a pioneer. It was through Ramiro Morris that the Assemblies of God work with the indigenous people began in the country of Panama.

Ramiro dictated his story to us in Spanish and we then published the book "Había un Indio". In order to put his story into English, we have changed a few words for better understanding, but hopefully still captured the feeling and passion as it was told to us. It is his story, as he remembers it, and lived it.

Our prayer is that as you read his story, you will be inspired, motivated, blessed, and at the end of your life, **YOU** will also be able to say, **"It was all in the plan of God!"**

Janice & Richard Larson

CHAPTER 1

My name is Ramiro Morris, and I am an Indian.

I was born on April 10, 1935 on the Island of Rio Tigre, one of the 365 San Blas Islands.

This is my story as I remember it. My father's name is Wilfred Morris and my mother's name is Emilia Diaz de Morris. I eventually came to know them, but that story comes later.

RESCUED

My father, Wilfred, spent many years living in Panama, away from the San Blas Islands. He met a man named Thomas Pio, a black man from Bocas del Toro, a province of Panama. They met in 1910, became friends, and one day they said, "Let's go to the United States of America."

So they found a boat and left for the United States in 1910. They did not have passports or any other papers for leaving the country, but were given a letter of recommendation by Doctor Porras, President of Panama. So they left in a sailboat.

They arrived in the United Sates and eventually left in a boat for Europe. While sailing past Canada, where there are a lot of icebergs, the boat ran into the ice. The boat was made of wood, and immediately started to sink. However, another boat came by and rescued them and took them to England.

In England, they began to haul cargo from England to Australia, passing by the continent of Africa. They continued this work for several years.

Once, on one of their trips back, passing by Africa, and getting close to Spain, they ran into a big rock and the boat sank. But again, they were rescued.

I WAS ON THE BEACH OF THE ISLAND

World War I started in 1914. Years passed and in 1927, they returned. My father returned to the San Blas Island of Comarca Cuna and Mr. Thomas Pio returned to Bocas del Toro. Mr. Thomas Pio married Marta Castro and her name became Marta de Pio.

On the island of San Blas, Emilia (who was going to be my mother) was alone because her first husband had died. He was burned in an accident in the river Atrato. She had three children at this time.

She married Wilfred Morris, and with my father had four more children. I was born April 10, 1935. I remember being on the beach of the island.

"HERE HE IS, TAKE HIM WITH YOU"

In 1943, my father again left the island and returned to the city of Colon, where he met up with the same Mr. Thomas Pio. They began to haul cargo from Bocas del Toro to Colon.

One day Mr. Thomas asked my father, "Wilfred, how many children do you have?" My father said, "I have five sons and two daughters." My father asked Mr.

Thomas, "How many children do you have?" He answered, "I don't have any. My wife was pregnant two times but none lived."

Mr. Thomas then said, "Well, we have been friends for so many years; why not give me one of your children?"

My father went and found me, and brought me to Mr. Thomas. "Here he is – take him with you!" There were no papers or witnesses to this transaction. That is how I got to Puerto Limon in Costa Rica (Costa Rica is the country located to the north of Panama) in the year 1945-1946. I was ten years old!

The place was called Punta Mono, a land with mountains, cows, chickens and more. I grew up in this place. There was no school, but Mr. and Mrs. Pio said they were going to make me their child, and they also said they would educate me.

But they didn't. Their parents were 70 years old and needed help, so it became my responsibility to take care of them, their animals, chickens and everything.

I ACCEPT CHRIST AS MY SAVIOUR

In 1953, I was a young man, working in the sugarcane fields. Missionary David Kensinger and missionary Louis Spencer came to Talamanca for a three-day evangelistic campaign. The third and last day of the campaign, I accepted Christ as my Savior. Juan Paddyfoot was the pastor.

My mother and father did not know that I had become a Christian. They were Catholics and I was hiding the fact that I was now a Christian.

But my foster sister loved to dance and said to me, "Ramiro, a band is coming from San Jose and we don't want to miss the music. Let's go!" I was young and I loved to dance too. She said to me, "Are you a Christian now?"

But I didn't answer her a word.

The next day I told her, "You need to forgive me. I have always listened to your counsel, but today I can't do that. I'm not going with you to the dance. I am going to go in a different direction."

She got mad at me and said, "Don't be so dumb! I thought that the Indians from San Blas Islands were smarter than that! Why have you done this? Ok, I'm going to tell your mother that you are a Christian now."

I went to see pastor Juan Paddyfoot. He was already on the platform of the church. I grabbed his hand and said, "Brother Juan, please pray for me because my sister is going to accuse me of being a Christian."

At the end of the service, about 9:00 PM, I returned home to Puerto Viejo and that was when everything started to happen.

"PACK UP YOUR CLOTHES AND LEAVE"

I arrived home about 11:00 PM, but nothing happened. In the morning, I left for work and everything was fine. I returned home to eat at 3:00 PM and then got ready to leave for church. Now my sister was awake. But God does everything correctly and good.

My other foster sister was there in the house. My mother looked at me – I was cleaned up to go to church – and she said, "You think you're a real man now and don't want to obey us anymore now that you are an Evangelical."

She continued, "The Evangelicals are of the devil, because they enter by the window instead of the door. The Catholics are legitimate, because God told Peter that he was going to be the church, and the first Pope, and enter through the door. The Evangelicals enter through the window and are thieves. They are of the devil! If you don't want to be with us, pack up your clothes and leave!"

I took my clothes and was preparing to leave, when Marta, my foster sister said to me, "Ramiro, I have my own house now. Go and take care of things and then you can come and stay and eat at my house."

She continued, "The only thing that I am going to say is that Mother and Father raised you. They can't help you in any way now, but please come everyday and do the work for them. I'm a Jehovah Witness, but you can stay with me."

I was about 20 years old and was a man now. I could go out and get a job, and in fact others had offered me jobs. Now she was telling me that I needed to come and work again every day, even if they had thrown me out of the house.

I thought to myself, "No, I'm not going to do it!" I packed my clothes and prayed, "Lord, what should I do?

Father, what should I do?" I heard a voice behind me saying, "Obey Marta!" I heard the voice three times and I thought, "Oh Lord, again?"

In the morning, I went there to work and said, "Good morning Mother. Good morning Father." Neither one spoke a word to me. For two years, I continued going to church and working really hard for them. I would greet them, "Good morning", and for two years they never said a word to me.

CHAPTER 2

TIME TO LEAVE

Finally, the time came when I heard the voice of God telling me it was time for me to leave.

I owed some money – 800 colones – because I had had a baby with a woman there. I owed her the money. Now I said, "Dear Father, help me to finish paying all that I owe. When I pay all that I owe, then I can leave with you, Heavenly Father."

I had made this promise, not with a man, but with the Lord, and I was going to fulfill it. The cacao harvest came, and I cut more than 300 boxes of cacao plants. I paid my debt and had 20 colones left over.

Now the Lord said to me, "Go and ask forgiveness from your Mother and Father." "Why should I ask them for forgiveness, Lord? I haven't done anything to them!" Three times came the word of the Lord, and I had to obey!

In the afternoon, I went and asked them to forgive me. I said, "Good afternoon Mother and Father." They did not say a word to me. I said, "This is the last time you are going to see me. I am leaving here now."

My mother started to cry. They said to me, "Son, son, you don't have to ask us for forgiveness. We are the ones who need to ask you to forgive us. These two years we have seen that you are a different Ramiro. You have changed, and now you are a new Ramiro. This new Ramiro has come and worked and done the work very, very well!" They continued crying and saying, "Forgive us! We are of the devil, not you!"

Although I did not understand any of this, I could see the hand of God, and how He was working in all of this.

"ARE YOU DRUNK?"

So I left their home and went to my house. I had worked for the Petroleum Company and they had paid me a Panamanian monthly wage of $380.00 balboas (dollars) and that was a lot of money in those days. I had a lot of clothes - three suitcases full. I changed clothes two or three times a day.

I went to my neighbors in the city of Puerto Limon and said, "Come here – here are some clothes." They said, "Ramiro, are you drunk or crazy? Where are you going?" I said, "I don't know where I'm going."

In those days, I was very strong because I had lifted weights, and practiced boxing, etc. I had a real good strong body. Again they said, "Are you sure you are not drunk?" "No!" I said, "I'm not drunk. I'm leaving tomorrow. Here, take the clothes. They are for you." I gave the dishes and kitchen things to a lady who had helped me a lot.

This is how things happened, and I was left with only one pair of pants, one shirt, and my Bible. The people said to me, "You were raised here with us and now, where are you going?" Again I told them, "I don't know!"

THE BLESSING FROM MY PARENTS

I had asked my mother and father to forgive me, but the next day I went to them to say goodbye. My mother said to me, "Who is going to bury me or put me in the grave? You are the only child I have. I don't have any other children, only you. I will need you to bury me." "I don't know, but I'm leaving now," I told her.

Here is the blessing. They said to me, "Ramiro, you don't want to hear anything, but may God bless you wherever you go in this world!" This was the blessing from the two of them.

I left walking.

I WANT TO KNOW GOD!

I walked until evening when I came to a house. A woman was in the house, and I asked her, "Can you give me a place to sleep tonight?" She said to me, "Where have you come from? Are you a thief? Have you killed anyone?"

"No!" I told her. "I haven't killed anyone! No! I'm not a thief! Look, I have this Bible and it's a black book and I want to know the author of this Bible. I want to know God, and because of that, I'm following Him."

She asked me if I had eaten any food, and I told her, "No, I haven't eaten anything." She gave me a meal of beans, rice, and chicken, and in the morning a good breakfast. I prayed for them, and left walking until I came to the town called Pensar.

THIS IS HOW IT ALL STARTED

In the city of Pensar, I would need to cross the river in a boat. I had a friend, who had worked with me at the Petroleum Company, and he said to me, "Ramiro, I'll pay your boat passage." "Good," I said.

He purchased a ticket for the boat, also for the train, and even some food. I arrived where my stepsister Marta lived. I was very dirty because I had been walking for two days. She washed my clothes, and I put them back on.

At three o'clock in the afternoon, I left the house and went to downtown Limon. When I got there, I found Machito, a Christian brother, and missionary David Godwin handing out tracts and invitations for an Evangelistic Campaign that evening. They were going to have a three-day Campaign. I said to brother Godwin, "Give me part of your tracts and invitations." I started handing them out all over the city of Limon, inviting people to attend the Divine Healing Campaign.

This is how it all started. A lot of people attended the Campaign, but not all of them accepted the Lord as their

Savior. Yes, God manifested His Glory, but only one person, named Alvaro, gave his life to the Lord. Yes, just one soul. But Pastor Paddyfoot came to Limon to be the pastor of just one person, and now in the Limon Valley, we have more than 80 churches and preaching points.

CHAPTER 3

I ARRIVE AT THE BIBLE INSTITUTE

The following day, I arrived in San Jose (the capital city of Costa Rica). I arrived by train, using the 20 colones that I hadn't yet used. My train ticket actually cost 18 colones. When I arrived in San Jose, I began walking and asking where the Bible Institute was located. I finally arrived at the Bible Institute in Moravia (suburb of San Jose) at 5 PM in the afternoon.

No one was at the Institute, except Mari, the wife of Marcos Murillo, the Superintendent of the Assemblies of God of Costa Rica. They lived on the property and she was there with her children. Sister Mari said to me, "There's no one here, but there is a storage room where you can stay. We don't have any food yet because my husband is gone preaching."

That night I was invited to testify at a church and they gave me an offering of ten colones. With the offering of ten colones, we were able to buy rice, beans, sugar, flour, meat, cheese and bread. We bought all of that because ten colones was a lot of money. It was sufficient for the Marcos Murillo family and for me. I stayed with the Murillo family for two or three month.

THE BIBLE INSTITUTE RULE

The Bible Institute rule was that they wouldn't receive or accept students who hadn't finished sixth grade. I hadn't had any schooling. No studies at all. The leaders of the Bible Institute had a meeting and decided to have patience with me. Missionary Ruth Kensinger said, "I want to change this rule." They prepared a literacy program for me. Sister Elba Baez took a lot of time to prepare me and help me learn to read and write.

When missionaries Richard and Janice Larson arrived in Costa Rica, I was in my first year at the Bible Institute. I didn't understand any Spanish. I only spoke the English spoken by the black people where I was raised. When the Bible speaks of "Mt. Zion", I didn't know what the word "Mt." meant, or where it was located. When the Bible says, "The Glory of the Lord fell", I didn't even understand what the "Glory of the Lord" meant. It was very difficult for me!

STARTING VARIOUS CHURCHES

Superintendent Marcos Murillo sent me, along with brother Ramon Rojas, to Buenos Aires, a city in southern Costa Rica. I was to be the co-pastor. We left San Jose and arrived in Talamanca. From there, brother Rojas and I, and another brother from Talamanca, crossed the mountains. We arrived in Buenos Aires - from the ocean to the Central Valley. It took us four days to cross the mountains in the cold.

In this place, I began planting pineapple in order to earn money to go back to the Bible Institute. I stayed there almost a whole year working with the pineapple and earned money for my school bill.

In Costa Rica, I started various churches. Brother Marcos Murillo had taken me to Rio Cabagra, and there I began an almost new work.

Brother Marcos Murillo brought missionary Larson to visit me there. In order to get to this place, they had to travel almost six hours in Land Rover, and then by mule in the cold, fog, and mist of the mountains. At night you could see the people come walking from all over the mountains, with lamps in their hands, through the fog and mist, just to come to church. I was their pastor!

Sometimes, when we had conferences in the city of Palmar Norte, I had to walk from my church because I didn't have any money. The distance from Buenos Aires to Palmar Norte was 51 kilometers. In all of this, I lived by faith, because that was the teaching I received.

Missionary David Kensinger said to me, "Brother Morris, I'll help you when I can, but it's not always possible. Don't look to me! Look to the one who called you, ask Him only!"

This is the teaching that missionary Ralph Williams, another great servant of God, gave me. He told me, "I wait on God, and it doesn't matter if I have or don't have, I depend only on Him. He has brought me everything. One time I was with the missionaries and didn't have anything to eat. But, even if it was only water and bread, I have always eaten!"

Missionary David Kensinger once said to me,

"Brother Morris, when the first missionaries started, they started with nothing. The missionary movement was born in the United States, and the missionaries have gone to all parts of the world."

THIS MESSAGE SPOKE TO ME

I loved how missionary Ruth Kensinger preached, and the following message helped me greatly. She told a story from Africa, about an Indian who was going to kill missionaries with arrows. When the Indian arrived where the missionaries were, he found three men dressed in white surrounding the missionaries, and the Indian left without using his arrows.

That night in a church, the Indians listened to a sermon and when the invitation was given, they gave their lives to the Lord. Later the Indians attended the Bible Institute to study the Word of God. They graduated from the Institute and then returned to their village and won the whole village to the Lord.

I thought, "I'm an Indian, but I prefer to preach and start churches in Talamanca and other parts of Costa Rica." I felt that I was Costa Rican and didn't feel at all that I was a Kuna Indian from the San Blas Islands in Panama. No, I had nothing to do with the Kuna Indians. But, this message spoke to me.

CHAPTER 4

"REMEMBER THAT YOU ARE PANAMANIAN"

Because I spoke English, I was able to speak to the missionaries that were studying Spanish at the Language School in San Jose, Costa Rica. The Larsons invited me to their home to take care of their kids, and missionary Godwins did the same. We began to know each other and pray together.

After four years in Costa Rica, where they had planted a new church, the Godwins were now on their way to the neighboring country of Panama, with plans to open the first Assemblies of God church there. Brother Godwin said to me, "Brother Morris, remember that you are Panamanian. You are from there." The Larsons, and missionaries Palsers, told me the same thing. God was calling me to Panama.

Brother Godwin began the Campaign to start the new church in June 1967, and the church was growing quickly. He had prepared a movie that showed the new work, and also showed pictures of the Kuna Indians from the San Blas Islands. I began to say, "Look – these are my people! My mother and father are like this." My heart was moved, and I said, "Lord, like the Indian from Africa who was able to win many souls, use me as I go and work with the missionaries in Panama!"

"NOW YOU DON'T OWE US ANYTHING MORE"

The Larsons were ready to leave Costa Rica and move to Panama, but they told me I should go later. Finally the time came for me to leave.

I had studied for three years at the Bible Institute but had not paid my tuition. I owed the tuition. Brother Gilbert, from the school was always saying to me, "When are you going to pay your bill?" I didn't want to call my family, because they had told me to leave home, and I didn't want to bother them.

I went to the cafeteria to pray. "Lord, when am I going to pay it?" I had worked cutting coffee in order to make enough money to eat something at the Bible Institute, but one morning brother Gilbert called me and said, "Brother Morris, come here. Sign here!" I signed and he said to me, "Now you don't owe us anything more"

He handed me 200 colones. I didn't have any clothes, so with those 200 colones I bought two shirts, two pair of pants, and packed my tiny suitcase.

I'LL JUST START WALKING

Now I was left with no money. Early in the morning, in the cold, I said to the Lord, "Father, what shall I do? How am I going to go to Panama? I don't have any money, Lord, not even five cents! What am I going to do?

Well, I'll just stat walking!"

In the morning, Superintendent Marcos Murillo, Assistant Superintendent Báez, and missionaries Kensingers and Brookes, all arrived at the Bible Institute. They all came. I said to them, "Brothers, I've decided to go to Panama and I want to say goodbye." They didn't answer me.

I started walking, leaving the Bible Institute, on my way to a little store that was owned by a Christian brother. Suddenly, brother Báez called me. "Brother Morris, brother Morris, come here!" I came back and brother Báez said, "Where are you going?" I answered, "I'm going to Panama now." He said, "Do you have any money?" I told him, "No, I don't have any money." "Don't be crazy," said brother Báez. "Do you think that Panama is right around the corner?" I said, "Brother, I am willing to walk!"

I was probably crazy, but I believed that the Holy Spirit and the Spirit of God did this in order that the brothers would help me. I didn't understand anything that God was doing until many years later. "I'm walking." "No!" they said, and got out 100 colones. The ticket from San Jose to the Panamanian border cost me 100 colones.

I WAS A MAN WITHOUT A COUNTRY

When I arrived at the border, I couldn't cross. I wasn't a Panamanian. I wasn't a Tico (Costa Rican). I didn't have papers from any country. I was a man without a country. The year was 1968 and Omar Torrijos had become the leader of Panama. There was a strike going on, with a lot of police, and no one could cross the border.

I started walking to the Costa Rican city of La Cuesta and found pastor Francisco and the church service was already in progress. Pastor Francisco said to me, "Brother Morris, come here to the platform. Where are you going?" I told him, "I'm going to Panama but I can't cross the border." The pastor asked his congregation, "How many Panamanians are here tonight?" There was a big group. The pastor said, "Take brother Morris the other way, crossing over the mountains to the border." And they did!

After crossing the border, I boarded a bus that was going to the city of David, in the province of Chiriquí, Panama. But, I didn't realize that the bus had to cross the boarder again. The guards stopped the bus and the boarder agent said, "Everyone get off the bus!" Everyone got off the bus to show his or her papers, except me.

I stayed on the bus, and I don't know if they didn't see me, if God made me invisible, or what, but they checked the papers of everyone and didn't say a word to me. This happened seven times before we got to David.

When we got to David, I had a thousand tracts with me and I began to preach and give out the tracts. Someone came and said, "Where have you come from?" I answered, "I've come from Costa Rica."

IT WAS ALL IN THE PLAN OF GOD!

I was in David and was going to leave for a city named Santiago. I made a final call to missionary David Godwin who lived in Panama City, approximately five hours away. I was still living on 35 colones.

A young man came and sat next to me on the bus. He asked me, "Do you know Panama City?" I told him, "It's been years since I've been there – it was in 1943." He said, "Do you know where the bus stops?" "No, I don't know," I said. The young man said, "Well, when we arrive in Panama City, you can follow me and I'll take you to the Hotel Ideal." I said, "Well, I don't know, someone is going to be waiting for me."

When we arrived in Panama City, I followed him until we got to the Hotel Ideal. I saw a car there, but didn't know why it was there. I crossed the street and called brother Godwin again. He asked me, "Where are you?" "I'm at the Hotel Ideal," I said. Brother Godwin answered, "Good! Brother Larson left home at 9 PM to pick you up and he should be there. But if not, tell the lady at the Hotel desk to give you a place to sleep, and I'll come in the morning to get you."

At that moment, I saw the car again and pounded on the window. It was brother Larson who was waiting for me. It was now one or two in the morning. But it was all in the plan of God!

CHAPTER 5

"LOOK FOR YOUR FAMILY"

But the story doesn't end here. I was with the missionaries almost a whole year before going to Comarca Tacamaca (the San Blas Islands.) During that year, I helped missionary Larson by going door to door in the Canal Zone; inviting people to attend the new English speaking church they were starting. I also helped missionary Godwin in the new Vista Hermosa church in Panama City and missionary Palser in the new church in the city of Colon.

One day, one of the missionaries said to me, "Brother Morris, go find your family." I started looking at the San Blas Indians that lived in Panama City, because there were many living there. I thought, "How am I going to know them?" I searched and searched, asking if they knew anyone from Rio Tigre. They said, "Yes, there is someone from Rio Tigre." It was my uncle. I asked him, "Are my mother and father alive?" "Yes, yes, they are alive."

I sent my parents a letter, and then had a meeting with the missionaries to get money to leave. Between all of them, they gave me enough for my airline ticket, which cost me eight dollars, and something for food. In the letter, I told them I was coming there, and wondered how I could make contact with them. The airplane would be landing on the Nargana Island because Rio Tigre, where they lived, didn't yet have a landing strip.

I arrived about 2 PM in the afternoon, and there was my father. I more or less was able to recognize him because I had a picture of him. I said, "This is my father!" But I didn't know my mother. It had been years since I had seen her. She had a handkerchief, and when she saw me come out of the plane, she started to cry. She came and hugged me.

"THE LOST ONE HAS RETURNED"

In order to get from the Nargana Island, where the plane landed, to the Rio Tigre Island, we had to travel by cayuco (canoe). For me, it was the first time to travel by cayuco. It was a trip of almost one hour and I was very afraid.

When we arrived later in the afternoon to Rio Tigre, a lot of people were waiting to see me. They were talking and talking, and I didn't understand a word of their language. It was gibberish – completely incomprehensible to me. A cousin of mine was there and he spoke Spanish, so he helped interpret so I could speak with my mother. My father spoke English so I could speak to him.

In the following weeks, people came from many different islands to see me. It seems they were thinking, "The lost one has returned."

NO, I'M NOT GOING TO TAKE IT!

I was praying and praying because I wasn't used to the food and I got very sick. I became very thin. One night, in a dream, I saw my mother get up and bathe. She put on her suit, her necklace that she had to wear, and went to get some medicine for me, from an uncle of mine who was a "fortune teller." In the dream, I saw my mother make coffee and put a powder in the coffee. I saw it all in the dream.

After a while, I woke up and said to myself, "What is this?" Now that I was awake, my mother went to bathe and make my coffee. I thought, "This is wrong! It's just like I had seen in my dream."

My mother returned and brought me a cup of hot coffee, just like I liked it. But I didn't take it. I threw it away, and she started crying. She told me that the "fortune teller" said that I was going to die, and if he says so, then I was going to die. Also, he told her that my blood was not well, and that I needed medicine in my soup or food. I told her, "No, I'm not going to take it!"

Now I couldn't eat anything in my mother's house. I had a brother-in-law and he made me breakfast. He brought me coffee with milk, and he made bread that I could eat. But in my mother's house I couldn't eat anymore. I was very, very sick for a month. I could not walk. I was so tired and had no strength. After a month, I said, "No, no, I have God!"

The island was pure coconut. One afternoon around 7 PM, I went to the part that was the point of the island, and sat down. There weren't any coconuts up in the palm trees. It hadn't rained for three months. The sun was extremely hot. The wind was blowing. I sat down and said, "Jehovah, God of hosts, I have seen many miracles in so many people. Lord, you have raised up so many people. You took me to Costa Rica to know your Word, and to know you, Lord, and I have come back to my country to do the work that you have told me to do, and now they tell me that I am going to die?"

I kept praying, and it was about eleven o'clock at night when a drop of water fell on my forehead. Soon the water was all over me. I thought, "Where is the water coming from because it isn't even raining." I got up and I was well! I walked! Yes, I even jumped! Then I screamed, "Glory to God! Hallelujah, Lord! You have done this miracle, Lord. Here I am Lord!" Just a little drop of water and I received my miracle.

I returned home content, and knelt and prayed and went to bed, and rested. I slept calmly. In the morning I wanted something to eat, and I went to my brother-in-law's house and said, "I'd like you to make me oatmeal with milk." He went and bought an egg, added some bread, and I ate breakfast. At noon I wanted soup and he found a fish and made soup.

In the afternoon, I went to the Congress (a meeting of the caciques - chiefs). I sat at the Congress and they told me, "Don't they say that you are going to die?" I said to them, "No, I'm not going to die! I've come to see my uncle." My uncle was just coming in and I said to him, "Uncle, you say that I'm going to die, but I'm not going to die! Here I am! God gave me a miracle and He healed me! Here I am!"

After a few months, or maybe a year, my uncle got sick, and he called me to pray for him. I went and prayed for him, and he was truly healed. People were calling me to pray.

CHAPTER 6

THE WORK BEGINS

Thus began the work on the island of Río Tigre. There was already a Baptist church on the island, and they didn't want another church. I was already holding church services, but I couldn't get permission to start the church.

I called brother Godwin and said, "I need help!" So he sent brother Larson to have a meeting with the caciques (the chiefs.) But God is everything and everything was in God's plan. Brother Larson came and stayed with me for two days. The chiefs wanted to know if I had a boss, because this is how they think. I said, "Yes, I have the missionaries."

The Kunas love and have great respect for the North Americans, because the North Americans have helped them a lot in years past. The chief said, "The pastor of the Baptist Church is not from the island of Rio Tigre, he is not from our Island. Years ago they put up a school, and many people from our Island have studied and left for many parts of the world to be lawyers, doctors, engineers, and captains. Now Ramiro has studied so that he can do the work of the Assemblies of God here.

Missionaries Godwin and Larson came to the island for another meeting with the chiefs. The chiefs asked for an explanation and then said, "There is already a church here. How are we going to divide the members between one church and another?" The missionaries said, "No, no, this is not your job. The people that God touches, through the ministry of brother Morris, are the ones who will be in this church. And those who want to be Baptists can be Baptists."

In the evening, we attended the Congress where the missionaries preached, and my cousin Willis interpreted. This is how the Assemblies of God began here on the Island of Rio Tigre.

I started by having meetings with the children.

I MUST LEARN THEIR CUSTOMS

Those on the Island didn't understand me at all yet. I asked the Lord, "How do I do it? I must be with these people. I came to be a spokesman." The thought came, "I must learn their customs and traditions."

I learned quickly. "If I don't know their customs, how am I going to preach? They won't understand me."

Now, the same words and thoughts they use, I also use, and apply them the same way the Bible does. That way, they were able to understand me.

I stayed several years like that. The whole Comarca region was looking to me. "Where is Ramiro? Where is he? He now gives us advice." (Now I was in Panama City). God did a special work and the honor and glory belongs to God. The people said, "There is no other like Ramiro!"

One other thing: they invite me to help them when they need help. We have helped a lot. Here on the Island, some houses burned. The people were left without clothes, without food, without anything. But the churches in Costa Rica collected money, and other people helped a lot as well, to help these people. Now the people look to us. I see what God has done. Before they rejected me, but now they look to me.

CHAPTER 7

"MARRY SOMEONE FROM YOUR OWN PEOPLE!"

I was now looking for a wife for myself. But on the San Blas Islands, it's not that way. There, the mom and dad look for a husband or wife for their son or daughter. But I was doing it wrong. I liked a girl from the Baptist Church. She was a good girl, who sang and was a teacher. I needed someone to help me with the children.

Since I had been living outside of the San Blas Islands for so many years, when I arrived my mother said to me, "Ramiro, do not go fishing, or go to the mountains to work. Don't do anything! Nothing, nothing! You stay here and we will work in your place." I stayed a year without working. But who is going to marry a lazy man?

They look for men who work, and the father and mother of the girl from the Baptist church said, "Not to him!" I looked at another girl and not that one either. I said, "It's okay. In Costa Rica there are many single Christian ladies. I will return to Costa Rica."

When I decided that, I went to Panama City and missionary Rafael Williams told me, "Brother Morris, I have worked with the indigenous people a long time in other countries, and I want to say, 'Don't do that!' You must marry someone from your own people! If you marry someone from Costa Rica and you go back to the island, she will not be received. They will only receive you, but they will reject her." He told me that if you marry your own people, you will both be received, and by the chief too. And I had to obey.

"HERE SHE IS"

Now one afternoon, my father came to me and said, "Son, a man called me and said, 'I have a daughter and I am looking for a husband for her. I want it to be your son.'"

He had looked at two other men but neither one wanted to marry her. The man said, "I understand that pastors have to spend time taking care of their church and don't have much time to work. I will not force him, but I want to give her to him." My father replied, "My son is not a boy or young man. He is a man now. He understands and you have to talk to him."

I went to where the man was and talked to him. He told me, "Here she is!" There on the island, when you promise to get married, you have to get married at once. Not two or three days later, but right away. But when my future father-in-law went to talk to the chief, the chief said, "Go and send me Ramiro."

When I arrived, the chief and my nephew were both there. The chief told me, "Here we have a law that when the man's mother and father meet the girls mother and father, they are to marry at once." But the chief went on to say, "but I will respect you. Because you didn't grow up here on the island, but you grew up outside, I'm going to give you three months of engagement. After these three months, you come and get married here. You have to get married here! But go, and tell your boss so he will know."

THREE MONTHS TO PREPARE EVERYTHING

I went to missionary David Godwin and he told me that because he was starting the new church and had meetings every night of the week, he didn't have time to go to the island and marry us. Missionary Larson didn't have time either. Missionary Palser didn't have time, but he told me, "I'll call my brothers who live in Indiana, North America. They will be coming within a few months." Three to five members of brother Palsers family arrived and they arrived in time so they could marry us.

But I was going to use these three months to go to Costa Rica. I was looking for a little money, an offering from the churches in Costa Rica. There they gave me a good offering.

I returned to Panama. When a member of the region marries, it is his responsibility to prepare food for all the people of the island. I had to buy a big pig. This pig cost me eighty dollars. It was very big. I also had to buy rice, four bags of rice, and macaroni to mix with the meat. The meat had to be well chopped and well done to mix it with the macaroni. They would eat breakfast, lunch and dinner on the day of the wedding. This was my responsibility. It wasn't much money, but thank God, I could do it all with a hundred dollars.

A north wind was blowing very hard the day they arrived by plane to marry us that night. We married in the traditional custom of the Comarca, first in the hammock and then in the Congress. My cousin interpreted the entire ceremony, and we were married.

Priscila was wearing all the gold around her neck – all the gold - and I put on my suit and tie and we were married in the Congress. Everything, everything, turned out to be so beautiful.

It was all God's plan, not ours. That was my marriage to Priscila. We already have over 44 years of marriage. The year we got married was 1969. I still am walking with Priscila.

We have had five children. The first child, *Elí,* was born and when he was about three years old, he became ill with pneumonia. The second son, *Esteban,* was only a few months old and got pneumonia too. I had no money and the hospital was eight hours away by boat. I had nothing, nothing, nothing!

LORD, EVERYTHING I HAVE IS YOURS

Eli, the first one died five days after getting sick. Esteban died six days after Eli. They both died the same week. This hurt my wife Priscila so very much. I felt it too. I didn't cry in front of the people. No! I went to the point of the Island, where at night when I was alone, I could cry and pray. I said, "Lord, what is this? Is there something I don't understand?"

But then I began to study the Bible, the book of Job, where Job lost everything. He lost his wealth, his children, and he lost everything he had. But Job said, "Everything I have is yours, Lord. I have nothing. Everything is the Lords. If you give to me, you can also take it away." I had to say the same thing, "Lord, everything I have here is yours. I only have your Spirit, Lord, which is in me, nothing more."

After that our daughter, *Loida,* was born. Later twins were born, although Priscila did not know at first that they were twins, she found out when they were born. But when they were born, one died and the other lived. The one who lived we named *Ronald,* who is already more than 37 years old. Then *Salugun* was born; his name is from the dialect.

ORIGIN OF RAMIRO MORRIS

Here is another story. It turns out that my grandfather grew up in England, and in England he was named Solomon Morris. But upon returning to the island, the Indians couldn't pronounce the name Solomon, so they changed his name to Salugun. In remembrance of my grandfather, I gave my son the name Salugun. I have told God that everything I have, I give to Him, and this includes my children.

CHAPTER 8

FREE FROM THE TRADITIONS

On the islands, the traditions are still very strong. However, there are many who are coming out very slowly. But you have to follow the traditions. It has cost me a lot! However, now my wife Priscila is free from all of this.

At first it was hard because I had to participate in the 'chicha' ceremony. (Chicha is an indigenous intoxicating brew of fermented sugar cane and coffee) One 'chicha' ceremony was done for my wife and another 'chicha' ceremony for our daughter. That was very difficult for me. Now things have changed for Priscila and everything is God first.

Once, my wife and I went to Costa Rica to the city of Naranjo. There I preached and Priscila prayed for the women, placing her hands on them and they fell under the power of the Holy Spirit. Thank God! Now things have changed. But it has cost me!

Missionary Bill Brooke said to me, "I admire you brother Morris, that you are still in the ministry! So many things have happened to you and it would have been so easy for you to leave the ministry. But, I admire you!"

THE DEWEYS BUILD A CHURCH ON RIO TIGRE

The Dewey Family, evangelists and musicians, from Nashville, TN, came every year to minister in Panama. They went to Rio Tigre and saw that our new work didn't have a building. We were just meeting under the trees.

The Deweys returned to America, went to a bank and took out a personal loan to build a building for the new Assemblies of God church in Rio Tigre.

The church that the Dewey Family built has a ceiling and was painted. It just lacks the flooring so we can put in the mosaic. Also, there is a brother from here in Panama who has helped us a lot.

MINISTERING TOGETHER

Priscila and I have traveled a lot. We have been in thirty-five states of the United States. Priscila is the only woman on the islands that has gone with the Kuna traditional dress (Mola, nose piercing and leg wrap). It is the first time in history that this was allowed. All Kuna women have to change their dress before going to another country, but Priscila is the only one who has gone with her Mola.

When we go to other places, and we are in a church service, she speaks in the dialect and I interpret. This has happened many times. Many people have accepted Christ through her.

INVITED TO GEORGIA

Priscila and I traveled to the state of Georgia. Ron Tyson, a man from a Baptist church, brought some Boy Scouts from the United States to the Canal Zone in Panama. They took several of these Boy Scouts in a boat out to our island. As Ron spoke only English, I was invited to speak to him. We became friends. He told me he was going to talk to the leaders of the Assemblies of God in Georgia, to invite me to their state. He invited me to visit Georgia.

It turns out that there were more than 500 farms in Georgia, and in this area was the estate of former President Jimmy Carter. They invited the farmers and more than 500 attended in the morning for breakfast, where I spoke to them.

The next day, pastors of the churches, even Catholic churches, came. On the last day, more then 200 government leaders in Georgia attended. A large platform had been constructed and I spoke and preached to them. I did not know why this was happening. Priscila was with me. They gave me twelve large boxes of all kinds of clothes. I was able to distribute clothes throughout the island and to other islands as well. They also gave me a chainsaw to cut wood and a motor. I also bought an engine.

CHAPTER 9

I'M GOING TO BE SHARK BAIT

Here is another story. I bought a boat engine and gasoline for $150, and then left in the boat by myself. I was a little more than eight hours from my island and had plenty of food, rice and clothes. That day the wind was strong and the sea grew rough.

I had been traveling for about two or three hours when the boat split in two. I lost everything I was taking, plus all the clothes, the food and the engine. Everything! Everything! Everything! I stayed in one little part of the boat. The sea came over me and I said to the Lord, "I have not even won a soul yet, nothing, and now I am going to be shark bait."

Then came four sharks with great fins. They came to where I was. When I saw them, I said to the Lord, "When am I going to feel the shark bites, Lord?" I was praying, praying and crying too. I did not know what I had done. I thought it might be a sin that had not yet come out of me.

In a little while, I began to hear the noise of a "swish, swish." There were two dolphins making noise and jumping on me. It was almost like they were talking to me. They were there a short time and left. I think they heard a boat coming in the distance.

There were sailors in the boat, and they told me that

the dolphins had come to the boat where they were, and were jumping and going round and round. It is said that when dolphins jump, they are signaling that something is happening. The captain said, "Something is going on. Let's follow them."

The dolphins came back to me and began to jump and spin around. Then they left. Soon, I heard that a boat was coming. I had a white shirt that I used to signal them and soon they came to rescue me. I was almost six or seven hours at sea. They rescued me!

IT DIDN'T TOUCH ME!

In Cabagra, the river had grown so large that I could not cross it. I had to sleep on a branch. It was very cold, but there I was, and there I stayed. In the morning, at dawn, when it was clear enough to see, I woke up and saw a large snake right at the top of my head. It was a very large snake. I got up and left very quietly.

Another night, when I could not cross a river because of how large it had grown, I had to sleep on the side of a road. When I woke up, I found a panther lying beside me. When I got up, the panther also got up and left.

Also, one day I fell asleep near a large river where there were many alligators, but they didn't do anything to me.

HAVE YOU SEEN ANGELS?

Someone asked me in an interview, "Brother Morris, I want to know if you have seen angels?" I said, "No brother, I've never seen angels. Only once did a man come that had a big face. He grabbed me, took me to a place and brought me back again to where I had been. Then I saw another man once when I ran out of food in Comarca.

One night, a sailboat from a small yacht, came to the island very late at night. A man came, knocked on my door and said, "Is Morris here?" "Yes, Morris is here." He was a tall, thin, young man, and he told me, "When I was buying food in a supermarket in Miami, I heard a voice that said, 'on the island where you are going, there is a man named Morris. Go back again and buy the same amount of food for him.'"

He arrived on the island and gave me the food. It was a very long and deep box filled with all kinds of food, and there was also an envelope with two hundred dollars in it. The people who were in the boat did not sleep on the island that night. I don't know where they slept. They came and gave me food and left. All this I have seen!

CHAPTER 10

DIFFICULTY IN SPEAKING

The church, Catedral de Vida (Cathedral of Life) in Panama City, has received me very well. The one who has been pastor for so many years is brother Ricardo Girón. When I returned to Panama, he was an adolescent and had problems speaking.

I would take him to his home after the evening church services because his mother would punish him for going to church. We had to walk from Vista Hermosa to Panama Viejo, a fairly long distance. After many years, God healed him of stuttering and brother Ricardo became pastor of that great church and helped me a lot.

WE ARE LOOKING FOR YOUNG PEOPLE LIKE YOU

I didn't win Edwin Alvarez to Christ, but the Lord was beginning to use me and this is the story.

One Sunday, in La Catedral de Vida, Edwin Álvarez's sister came and said, "Brother Morris, I know that God uses you. I believe this! I want to take you to talk to my little brother. My brother is studying law and wants nothing to do with God. I want to take you to talk to him.

I told her, "I'm going to preach tonight in Las Cumbres." She told me, "I'm going to bring you back here later." "No problem," I answered, and went with her,

They lived in Calle O in San Miguelito. When I arrived, he was sitting on a sofa, in white pants and no shirt. Sweating in the heat. He was listening to a cassette playing salsa music. His sister told him, "Lower your music a little! Brother Morris has come to meet you. I will go and prepare some food."

I didn't know what I was going to talk to him about. I had nothing, nothing, nothing in my mind to say to him. I greeted him and said, "I'm brother Morris. I am from Kuna Yala, but I grew up in Costa Rica, and now we are opening new churches here and we are looking for young people like you."

When I said, "We're looking for young people," like a flash it came to my mind to talk about Samuel. I said, "There was a prophet named Samuel, whom God used greatly in Israel. And God said to Samuel, 'Go to the house of Jesse and look for a son from the house.' Samuel took oil and everything necessary for anointing, and came to the house of Jesse.

When he arrived at Jesse's house, Samuel asked him, 'How many children do you have?' He showed him his children, and the children were already grown. Samuel asked, 'Do you have more?' 'Yes, I have one more out in the field, tending sheep.' Jesse said, 'Go and call him!' When the boy came, he was a blond boy and God said, 'Anoint him!' This was David, and he became the second king of Israel."

I told Edwin, "If you accept Christ as your Savior, God will use you here in Panama. Not only in Panama, but God will take you to the whole world." I prayed with him, nothing more. He did not accept the Lord, I only prayed with him. And I left.

Later, missionary Godwin told me, "Brother Morris, Evangelist Jeffrey is coming to have a campaign in San Miguelito. We are going to plant a new church. Come and help me." I did, and it was in this campaign that Edwin Alvarez accepted the Lord.

PTL CLUB IN NORTH CAROLINA

When missionary Juan Romero invited Priscila and me to North Carolina, I was able to meet David Wilkerson. Brother Wilkerson told me, "There is a lady here who wants to meet you. It is sister Kathryn Kuhlman."

We went to the room, and when my wife came in and sister Kuhlman saw her, she gave my wife a big hug. My wife was wearing all her gold - a lot of gold. We have a photo of this. This was at the PTL Club in North Carolina.

I also met brother Jim Baker and his wife. Then, sister Kuhlman came to me and said, "Pray for me." And I prayed for her. Then she prayed for me. I don't know much, and I don't understand everything, but people look to me to pray and there are so many testimonies. God has blessed many when I have prayed.

Afterwards, I began to think, "God, I am a sinner before you. How is this God?" But I remembered that great men of God had prayed for me too.

WE WILL GIVE IT ALL!

There was a meeting of more than 600 missionaries in Fort Worth, Texas. Priscila and I were there with missionary David Spencer, but missionary David Godwin did not know we were there.

The District Superintendent said, "We're going to collect a million dollars tonight. Tonight we will collect a million dollars for missions."

We didn't even have five cents because we were collecting money for Nicaragua, and nothing had been given to us personally, not even a nickel. But in my wife Pricilla's handkerchief there were two gold rings that had cost forty-five dollars each, and chains of our children who died. Each child had been given a gold chain.

Missionaries with their checkbooks were writing checks for fifty, one hundred or more. I had no money. I only had what was in the handkerchief. Priscila said, "We're going to give all this, it doesn't matter!" When David Spencer knew this, he told the missionaries, "I don't want to receive this. We will give the gold back again to sister Priscila." I said, "No, no, no!"

When they collected all the money, the Superintendent announced, "We have visitors here visiting us who have come from one of the Islands of Panama." Missionary Doris Godwin said the following to her self, "They have to be our missionaries. They must be ours. They don't have any money, but they are like the widow in the Bible. The widow gave everything she had, and this missionary couple, who work with indigenous people, don' have anything. But of what they have, they are giving to the work of missions."

Then they called us to the front and sister Doris shouted, "Glory to God! I knew that brother Morris was here." This testimony was published in a newspaper in Fort Worth, Texas.

I KNOW HOW TO LIVE AS PAUL SAID

Many things have happened to me. I have gotten quite discouraged. I was almost going to leave the work completely. The brothers in Costa Rica told me they were going to help me in the work and they hadn't helped me much. As the work in Panama was just beginning, they could not help much either.

We are praying for a house in Panama City. We only have one on the island. Priscila says, "When we go to other countries, we are treated so well. They give us food, and we have special rooms. How well they have treated us!"

I know how to live in poverty, and I know how to live as Paul said. Thank the Lord I could live in both places. I know someone else's hunger because I had it too.

When I go to some other place where I am invited, I also participate in giving, because I will receive too.

We are praying and are looking for a house worth thirty-two thousand dollars in Panama, in the area above Cabra. About five years ago, brother Roberto Williams said here in Panama, "Brother Morris is one of our pioneers of the work here in Panama; he is a pastor and he has nothing, not even a house. I suggest that we should look for a house for him." Everyone said "yes", but it didn't work out. Everything is in the hand of the Lord. Now my son is working, and his wife is working, and I said, "Well, any little thing that I receive, I will help too."

But the Lord takes care of everything. I don't have to worry about that. I remember that the missionaries used to say, "Here we have nothing, nothing, nothing, but we will have in heaven." Of course I got it, and many pastors have understood this. Some have sold farms and everything they have. But then I saw that we were wrong. I believe that we should have something on earth for the family, and in heaven too.

I have returned many times to see my family in Costa Rica. I have never forgotten them.

CHAPTER 11

CHURCHES AMONG THE INDIGENOUS PEOPLE

In Panama City, we have three churches among the indigenous people. In Comarca, we have four works, and they are asking for more.

Both Victor and Jaime have gone to the Bible Institute to prepare themselves for the ministry, but I could not help them with finances to continue their studies. The Baptist Church is receiving money directly from the United States to help their ministers, but the Assemblies of God could not help. It has been very difficult for them to prepare. But, thank God, the Assemblies of God is gradually gaining strength among the indigenous races.

Sister Green, a missionary from New Zealand, came to the island to help me. She came every year and brought food and clothes. Every time she came, she stayed three or four days. She even went to the house of my adopted father and mother in Costa Rica. She also went to the Comarca and met my real mother and father.

And now, that we are growing old, there is something else. I wasn't able to prepare many workers. But God is doing the work there. I also have my nephew who is working in the city of Colon where there is a church.

When my back was hurting a lot, brother Ricardo Girón, one of the officers of the Assemblies of God, said to me, "Brother Morris, you already have many years of being a pastor/missionary. It is now time to leave the pastorate. But you have freedom to preach where you want, but no longer a pastor.

They named brother Adolfo as pastor of the work.

THEY HAVE BEEN ON THEIR KNEES

The work here in Panama has grown so very much. There are already more than 800 churches under the leadership of Superintendent Lowell David. The men of God have been on their knees.

I have prayed on the sea and inside the sea for Panama. I have prayed in the Tuira River, a large river, in the province of Darién. I prayed in the mornings for all of Panama.

When I go past the volcano, and cross the high mountains, I say, "Oh God, Lord, bless Panama. Bless the nation, Lord. Bless the nation of Costa Rica, Lord."

I have prayed and fasted for the islands. But there are men and women, not just this servant; there are many who are praying for Panama. The work has grown greatly. Thank God!

THERE WAS AN INDIAN WORKING TOO

What many do not know is that among the North American missionaries, there was an Indian working too. Many do not know this. It is true that the missionaries had a call to Panama, but God had a call for me too.

The truth is, that the Assemblies of God of Panama was born in La Comarca in 1935, when I was born. Although, when I accepted the Lord as my personal Savior, I did not know anything about who the Assemblies of God or the Baptists were.

I only know that I accepted the Lord Jesus Christ as my Savior and powerful God. This is whom I accepted. I did not accept any earthly church, but after five or six years, I took the Assemblies of God as my base. GOD HAS DONE ALL THIS!

All this that we are expressing in this story was God's plan. It was God's plan that my father meet this black man, and that he give me to him. I grew up with these English speaking black people, and it was God's plan so I could know their language (English), although poorly spoken.

It was God's plan so I could know different customs: indigenous customs, customs of black people, and the customs of the missionaries. All this, so I could live and be part of all God was doing. God has done all this!

CHAPTER 12

(Words added by the author)

A BRIEF HISTORY OF THE BEGINNING OF THE ASSEMBLIES OF GOD OF PANAMA

THE GODWIN FAMILY

THE LARSON FAMILY

THE PALSER FAMILY

THE CEDERBLOM FAMILY

SUPERENTINDENT LOWELL AND ODILIA DAVID

THE FIRST ASSEMBLIES OF GOD CHURCH IN PANAMA CITY, PANAMA -1967

THE DAVID GODWIN FAMILY

The first missionaries of the Assemblies of God to Panama were David and Doris Godwin with their four children, Ron, Don, Dale and Cindy. Having just planted a new church in Costa Rica, they felt God's call to move to Panama and begin the work of the Assemblies of God there. Upon arriving in Panama, they rented a house and used one of the bedrooms as a radio studio. They recorded radio programs, putting them on local stations.

The Godwins invited evangelists Richard and Elva Jeffrey to help them start the campaign. The Jeffreys had planted many churches in Latin America.

The campaign began – in a tent - on June 13, 1967, and was designed to plant a new church. Hundreds of people attended and received salvation and healing. When it became necessary, they purchased a movie theater, and the church took the name of Temple Vista Hermosa – the area where they were located. In the revival environment, the first believers grew rapidly in their faith and became the first wave of workers to plant more churches.

The Godwins became the pastors of the new church and remained as pastors until January 1971, when they returned to the United States. Missionaries Richard and Janice Larson followed the Godwins and stayed on as pastors until 1976.

The Larsons built a new building and changed the name of the church to the Cathedral of Life. (Catedral de Vida). After six years, the Larsons left and the church elected Gregorio and Doris Campos as their first Panamanian pastors.

CANAL ZONE CHURCH – 1968

THE RICHARD LARSON FAMILY

In 1968, missionaries Paul and Elaine Palser and their family arrived in Panama, with the plan to establish a church in the Panama Canal Zone for English speaking people.

A building belonging to the Christian Science church was for sale, and the Palsers made the arrangements to purchase it. The building had been a courthouse, and had a panoramic view of the Albrook military base.

The Larsons were the first pastors of the Canal Zone church - for one year, 1969, followed by the Townsends, Hansons, Buenos, and others. In 1971 they began pastoring the Catedral de Vida (Cathedral of Life).

1968 - THE FIRST ASSEMBLIES OF GOD CHURCH IN THE CITY OF COLON

THE PAUL PALSER FAMILY

While the Palsers were preparing to start the church in the Canal Zone, they visited the city of Colon on the Caribbean coast. They found it was similar to the country of British Guyana, where they had just built a great church. The need in that city touched their hearts, and they located a building that was a large cinema to start their meetings. Hundreds attended the services and it was obvious that God was doing a great work.

The Palsers moved to Colon, leaving the vision of the church in the Canal Zone in the hands of the Larsons. The Palsers remained as pastors in Colon for four years. Then missionaries Wayne and Doris Turnbull and their family arrived, and eventually missionaries Richard and Sharon Ellis.

THE BIBLE INSTITUTES OF PANAMA

THE LARRY CEDERBLOM FAMILY

Of equal importance, was the opening of the first Bible Institute in the new church in Panama City and also one in Colon. The missionaries taught and prepared the first Panamanian ministers.

In 1973, the Cederblom family arrived to be the Directors of the Bible Institutes that were now opening throughout the country. They stayed for many years and did an excellent job in preparing ministers for the tremendous growth of the Panamanian Assemblies of God.

SUPERINTENDENT OF THE ASSEMBLIES OF GOD OF PANAMA

LOWELL & ODILIA DAVID

What has contributed to the stability of the work in Panama has been the leadership of Superintendent Lowell David. For more than forty years, brother Lowell has guided the work with wisdom and perseverance. Today, there is an Assemblies of God church in almost every community in the country. Thank you brother Lowell and sister Odilia!

*** Since the publishing of this book in Spanish in 2013, Superintendent Lowell David has passed on to his eternal reward.*

RAMIRO MORRIS & RICHARD LARSON
June 2012

BROTHERS AND FRIENDS FOREVER

JANICE (Juanita) LARSON WITH PART OF THE RAMIRO MORRIS FAMILY

June 2012

RAMIRO & PRISCILA MORRIS

2019

Made in the USA
San Bernardino, CA
19 November 2019

60103045R00042